AF583895

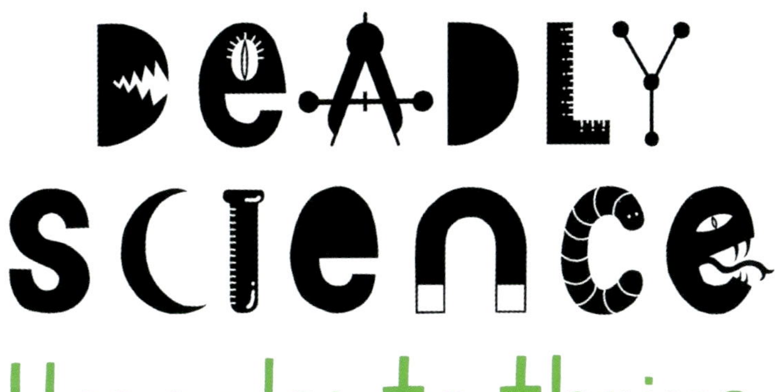

How plants thrive

Contents:

ADJUNCT ASSOCIATE PROFESSOR COREY TUTT OAM

DEADLYSCIENCE

DeadlyScience aims to provide Science, Technology, Engineering and Mathematics (STEM) resources to remote schools around Australia. So far, DeadlyScience has shipped more than 33,000 STEM books and resources to more than 800 schools across the country.

The organisation began when proud Kamilaroi man Corey Tutt found out that some schools in Australia were completely under-resourced and that Aboriginal and Torres Strait Islander children were discouraged from pursuing STEM because of this. DeadlyScience knows from personal experience that books and resources change lives and believes these kids deserve nothing but the best. Aboriginal and Torres Strait Islander peoples in Australia were the First Scientists of this land, and DeadlyScience is committed to preserving that history.

How plants thrive

A plant is a living thing that can produce its own food from water and carbon dioxide. Most plants that grow on land have two main parts – a root system that grows in the soil, and a shoot system (with a stem and leaves) that grows above the ground. Plants that grow in water have the same basic structure, but some float freely and have roots that dangle in the water and leaves that lie on the water's surface.

Handy plants

Plants (and their ocean relatives, the seaweeds) are essential for our survival. They produce the oxygen we need to breathe, the food we need to eat, wood we use for building, fibres to make cloth and paper, and even rubber to make tyres. Indigenous Australians have used native plants for food, shelter, medicine, tools and fibres for many thousands of years. Plants also provide food and shelter for wild animals, protect the soil from erosion, provide shade, cool the air, and remove pollutants from the air and from the water. Plants are very important to our existence, so we need to look after them, but what do they need to thrive?

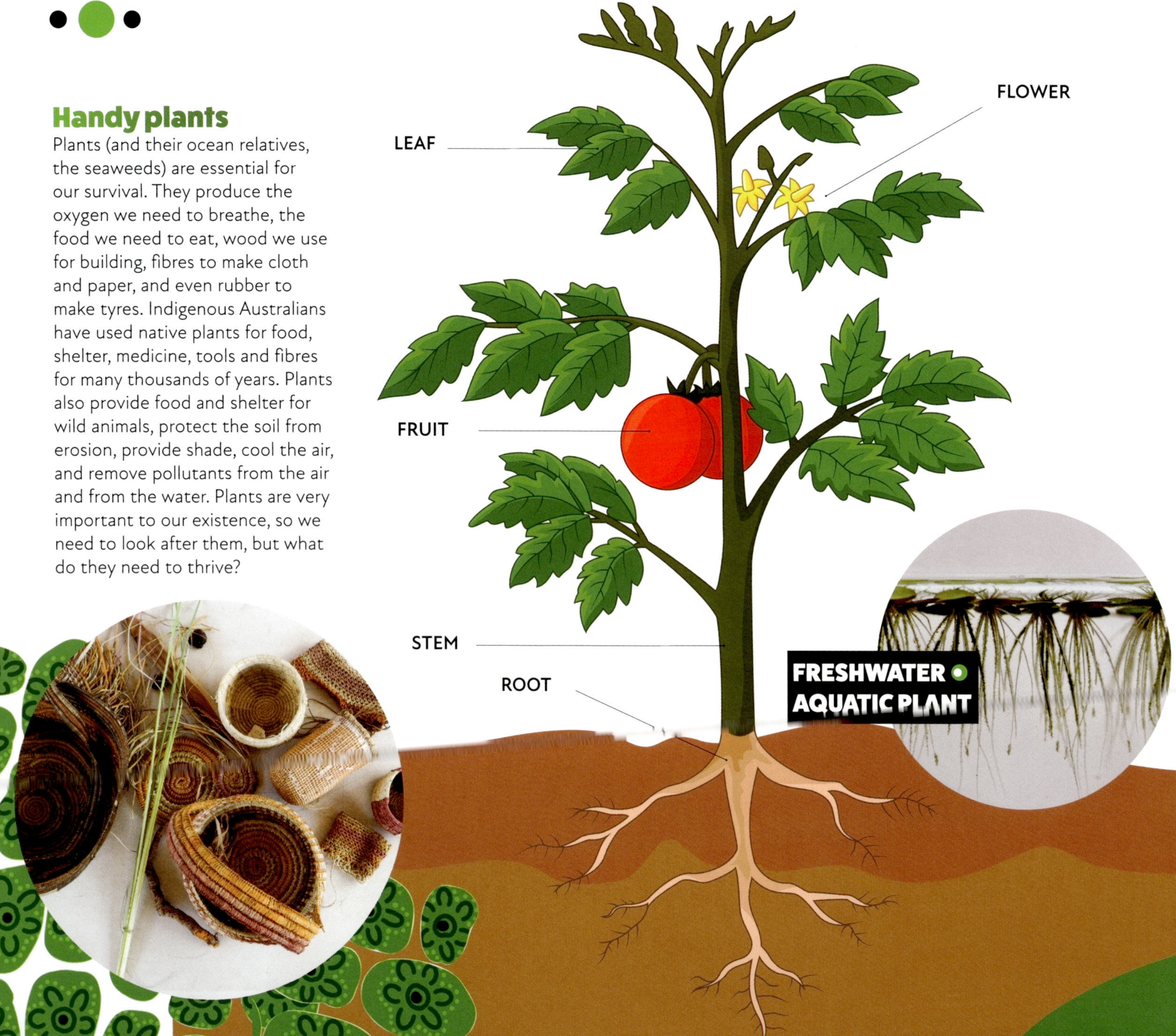

Bacteria

Some bacteria can also carry out photosynthesis. These bacteria are called cyanobacteria because of their blue-green colour ('cyano' comes from a Greek word meaning dark blue). Cyanobacteria are so small that they can only be seen clearly under a microscope, but they are important producers of food and oxygen in oceans, lakes and rivers.

DID YOU KNOW?

Long words in science are easier to understand if you break them into smaller words. The word photosynthesis is made up of 'photo', meaning light, and 'synthesis', meaning put together.

PHOTOSYNTHESIS

OXYGEN

LIGHT ENERGY

SUGAR

CARBON DIOXIDE CO_2

MINERALS

WATER H_2O

Survive and thrive

Plants need four main things to thrive – water, sunlight, carbon dioxide and nutrients. With these four essentials, plants are able to manufacture their own food through a process known as photosynthesis. In this process, energy from sunlight is used to combine carbon dioxide and water to produce sugars. The sugars can then be used by the plant to provide energy and building blocks for growth or can be stored for later use. An important by-product of photosynthesis is oxygen, a gas in the Earth's atmosphere that all animals depend on to survive.

FACT

A tree is estimated to absorb an average of 10–40 kg of carbon dioxide from the air every year!

Water

Most plants on land take up water from the soil. The water enters the plant's root system and is carried up to the leaves through vein-like tubes called xylem. Some of this water is used in photosynthesis and some is used to carry food made in the leaves to other parts of the plant through another set of tubes called phloem.

FACT

You can tell the age of a tree by counting the rings in its trunk. The oldest known tree is a bristlecone pine (*Pinus longaeva*) in California that is over 5000 years old.

XYLEM AND PHLOEM

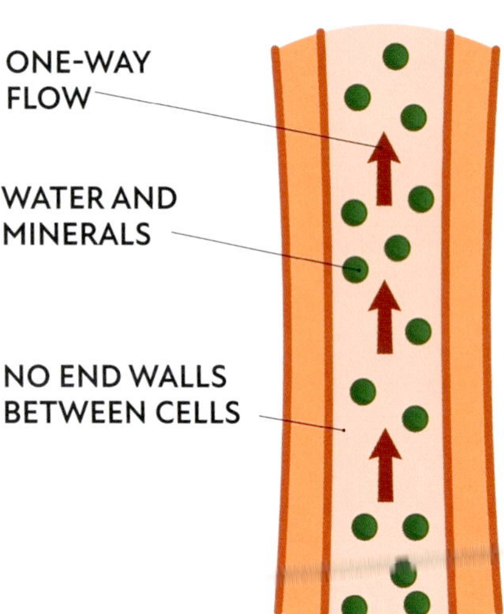

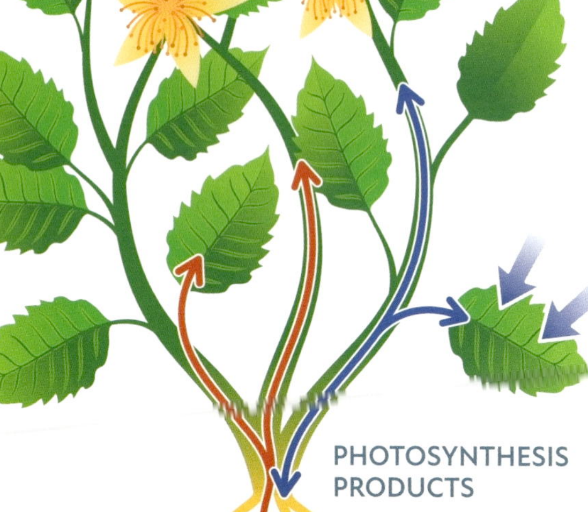

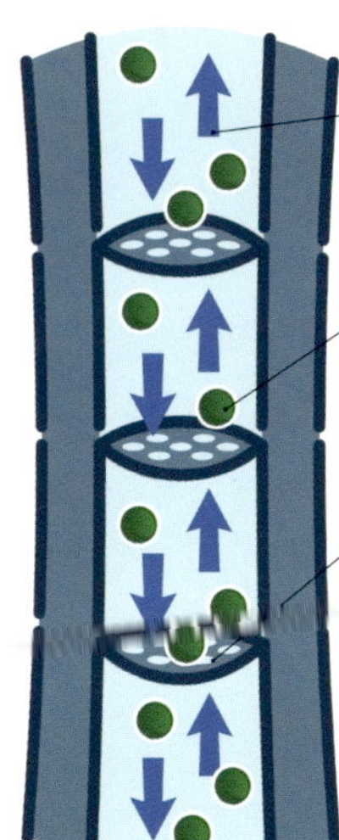

Woody plants

In woody plants, xylem forms a ring around the trunk, just underneath the bark. Each year, a new ring of xylem forms around the outside of the previous year's ring. Over time, these rings of xylem harden to form the wood that supports the plant as it grows taller. The water that travels through a plant is known as sap. Water travelling through the xylem contains mineral nutrients and is called xylem sap. Water travelling through the phloem contains sugars and is called phloem sap. Sap can be harvested from some plants for water, food or other uses.

YELLOW-BELLIED GLIDER

MAPLE SYRUP

DID YOU KNOW?

Maple syrup is made by tapping into the trunk of a sugar maple and draining its sap into a bucket. Just as we enjoy maple syrup, the yellow-bellied glider chews notches in gum and wattle trees to suck up sap.

Transpiration

Any water that isn't used for photosynthesis or to transport food evaporates into the air from the surface of the plant's leaves. This process is called transpiration. It helps to pull more water into the plant from the soil and is an important part of the Earth's water cycle. The amount of water a plant transpires is controlled by special openings in the leaves called stomata. (Stomata are described in the section on carbon dioxide.) When there isn't much water in the soil, the stomata close to stop water evaporating from the leaves.

TRANSPIRATION

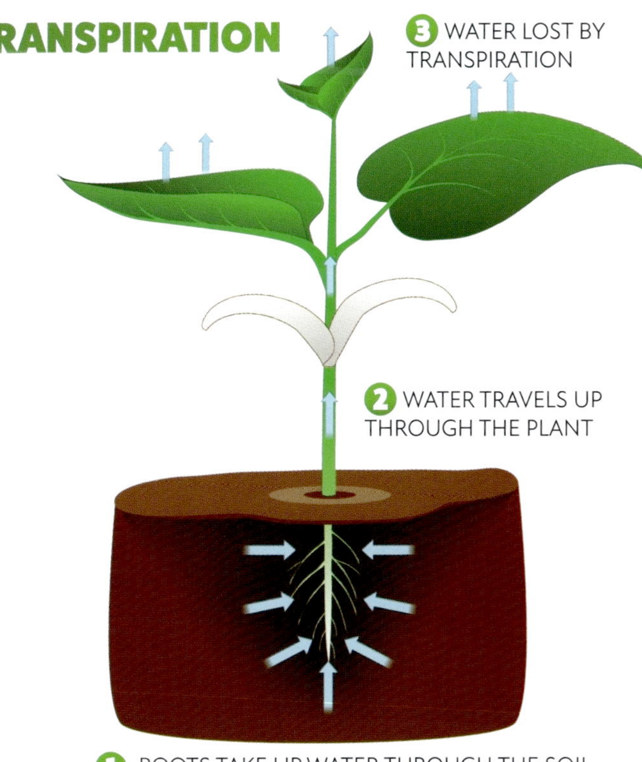

Dry conditions

Plants adapt in many different ways to help them survive when water is scarce. Some plants develop long roots that grow deep underground to find water. Some plants store water above ground in fleshy leaves or stems. Other plants store water below ground in their roots or special storage organs such as tubers. Some plants produce seeds that won't germinate until there is enough water in the soil for seedlings to survive. Some plants have even replaced their leaves with tiny scales to reduce water evaporation from the leaf surface.

PARROT-BEAK ORCHID

Underground storage

Greenhood orchids, such as the parrot-beak orchid, store water and starch in small underground tubers. The tubers (right) help the plant to survive underground through hot, dry summers. The Ngunnawal people dig up the tubers of this orchid to use as food.

COASTAL PIGFACE

In the Wudjari language of southern Western Australia, this plant's name is paainy.

Bottle tree

First Nations people carved holes in the soft bark of the bottle tree to extract the water stored within. The roots of the young plants can be eaten, and the fibre from the tree can be used to make nets.

FACT

The bottle tree (*Brachychiton rupetris*) stores water in its bottle-shaped trunk.

Coastal pigface

Coastal pigface is a succulent that stores water in its thick, fleshy leaves. The Noongar people of South West Western Australia crush the leaves of a similar pigface to make a medicine for treating stomach cramps and diarrhoea.

Kurrajong tree

The kurrajong (*Brachychiton populneus*) is a relative of the bottle tree. It is important to First Nations people as a source of food, fibre and water. The Ngunnawal people were able to extract water stored in the roots of this tree and also eat the roots, which are said to taste a bit like carrot.

DID YOU KNOW?

Tubers store water and food, so each 'eye' on a potato has a tiny bud that grows a new plant. First Nations people cultivated the tubers of the murnong or yam daisy (*Microseris* spp.) to eat.

Light

Plants absorb light from the sun through their leaves. Inside the leaves are special cells that contain a green pigment called chlorophyll. This pigment captures energy from sunlight that can be used by the plant to carry out photosynthesis. Chlorophyll is found inside the leaf cells in tiny round structures that are called chloroplasts.

FACT

A by-product of photosynthesis is oxygen, which humans need to breathe.

BIG SWAMP, BUNBURY, WA
To the Noongar Traditional Owners, the Bunbury region is known as Goomburrup.

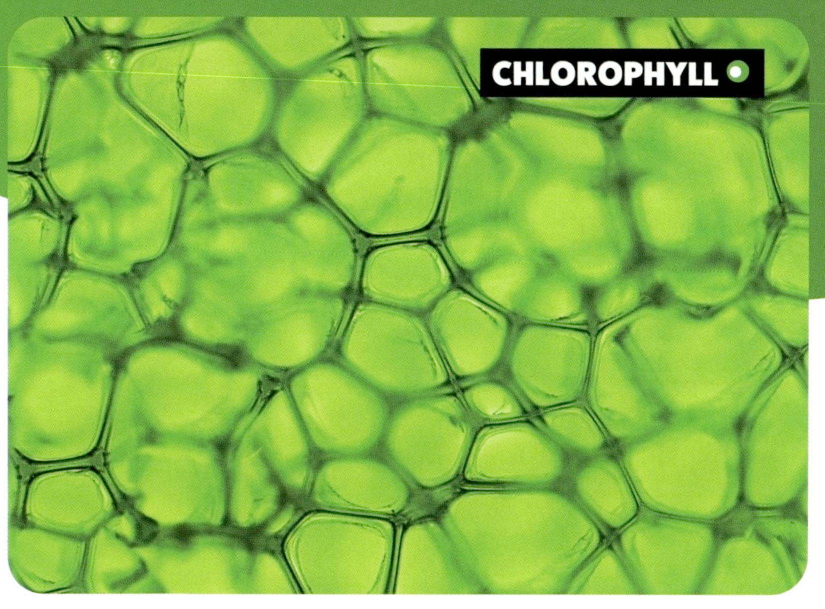

DID YOU KNOW?

A pigment is a natural substance that gives colour to plant or animal tissue; the word pigment comes from a Latin word meaning to paint. The word chlorophyll comes from 'chloro', meaning green, and 'phyll', meaning leaf.

Leaf shape

Plants have evolved different leaf shapes and arrangements, and different ways of growing, to capture as much sunlight as they can. One way they do this is by growing towards the sun. If a plant is shaded on one side but gets sun on the other side as it is growing, it will lean towards the sunny side to get more light!

Why plants are green

The light that comes from the sun looks white but is actually made up of many different colours. You can see these colours in a rainbow when the sun shines through water droplets in the air after a storm. Chlorophyll absorbs most of those colours but reflects green – this is why plants look green to our eyes!

Low light

Some plants grow where there is only a small amount of light. The rainforest floor is often dark because the tall trees above it block most of the sun's light. Plants growing in dim places may grow very large leaves to try to capture as much light as possible. Other rainforest plants have special adaptations, such as hooks or twining stems, which help them climb up and over other vegetation to reach more light.

RAINFOREST NEAR CAIRNS, QLD

Sleepy seedlings

Some rainforest plants produce large seeds to help their seedlings survive on the rainforest floor. These seeds have enough food stored to let the seedlings grow roots and shoots in very little light. The seedlings stay quite small, living but not growing much, until a storm or old age causes the trees above to fall and let in more light.

Golf ball seeds

The black bean tree (*Castanospermum australe*) is a rainforest species that produces seeds as big as golf balls. These seeds are prized by some First Nations Australians, including the Bundjalung people of northern NSW. However, the raw seeds are poisonous, so they need to be cooked, pounded, and then washed in running water for several days before they can be turned into flour and used to make damper.

DAMPER

BLACK BEAN SEEDS

DID YOU KNOW?

Some rainforest plants can survive as small seedlings for more than 30 years!

DID YOU KNOW?

Dugongs are more closely related to elephants than they are to dolphins, and they can eat up to 30 kg of seagrass a day!

DUGONG
To the Wunambal Gaambera people of the north-western Kimberley, this species is called balguja.

Underwater meadows

Seagrasses are flowering plants that spend their entire lives underwater, and Australia has more species than anywhere in the world! At least 27 of the world's 60 seagrass species grow in Australian waters, covering an estimated 20,000 km^2 of sea bed in Western Australia alone.

Seagrasses help oxygenate water, recycle nutrients, store carbon and stabilise sand. They are also important sources of food and shelter for marine life. Vast underwater meadows are crucial to the survival of the endangered dugong. Populations of dugong, which are sometimes called sea cows, graze on seagrass meadows in warm northern waters from Queensland's Moreton Bay, along the Great Barrier Reef, and Top End, over to the Kimberley and Shark Bay in Western Australia.

FACT
Plants that grow in the ocean – like seaweed – provide about 50–70% of the planet's oxygen, but roughly all of it is consumed by marine animals.

RED SEAWEED

DID YOU KNOW?

Sushi rolls are wrapped in sheets called nori made from a type of red algae.

Red seaweeds

Water at the bottom of the ocean can also be dark because some parts of sunlight don't travel well through water. Red seaweeds, which are actually algae but are close relatives of plants, can still grow in this environment because they have special pigments that help them absorb the parts of sunlight that can travel far into the water. Though red seaweeds also have chlorophyll, the other pigments cover up the chlorophyll and make the seaweed appear red. Some red seaweeds look almost black!

Carbon dioxide

Carbon dioxide (CO_2) is a gas that is found in the Earth's atmosphere. The amount of carbon dioxide in the air we breathe is very small compared to the amount of nitrogen and oxygen, but CO_2 is essential for photosynthesis. Plants on land absorb CO_2 from the air through special openings in their leaves called stomata. These same openings also allow water vapour and oxygen to be released into the air.

STOMATA AND GUARD CELLS

FACT

'Stoma' is a Greek word that means mouth. Stomata means more than one stoma.

On guard

Each stoma has a pore surrounded by two guard cells that control the opening and closing of the pore. During the day, when there is enough light for photosynthesis, the guard cells expand, causing the stoma to open and let carbon dioxide in and water vapour and oxygen out. In most plants, the stomata are closed at night, when there is no light for photosynthesis, which helps the plant to retain water. But stomata can also close during the day, when it is very hot or there is not much water in the soil, to stop the plant from losing too much water. When the stomata are closed during the day, the leaves can't take in carbon dioxide, so no photosynthesis takes place.

NATIVE PIGFACE

DID YOU KNOW?

Native pigface (*Carpobrotus rossii*) grows in coastal areas in dry, sandy soils and is known to take in carbon dioxide at night.

Dry climates

Some plants in very dry habitats use a special form of photosynthesis. These plants take in carbon dioxide at night so that the stomata can stay closed during the heat of the day. The carbon dioxide is changed into weak acids that can be held in storage compartments in the leaves (called vacuoles) until the morning. When the sun comes up and the plant can absorb light energy again, the carbon dioxide is released from storage and photosynthesis takes place. Plants that can store water in their stems or leaves (like pigface) sometimes use this form of photosynthesis.

PLANT CELL STRUCTURE

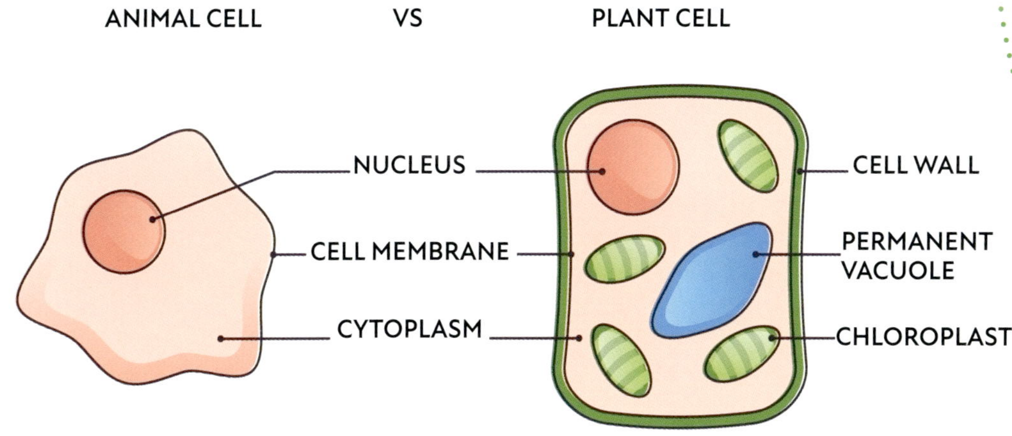

Nutrients

Plants get carbon, hydrogen and oxygen from carbon dioxide and water. But they need 14 other nutrients to thrive. Six of them – nitrogen, phosphorous, potassium, calcium, magnesium and sulphur – are needed in relatively large amounts, so they are called macronutrients. The others – chlorine, iron, manganese, boron, zinc, copper, nickel and molybdenum – are only needed in small amounts, so they are called micronutrients. These nutrients are present in the soil, attaching to soil particles and dissolving in soil water. Nutrients dissolved in water are taken up by the plant's roots and transported to the rest of the plant through the xylem.

FACT

Lightning makes nitrogen react with oxygen to form nitrous oxide. This dissolves in water to form nitrates, which fall to the ground inside raindrops.

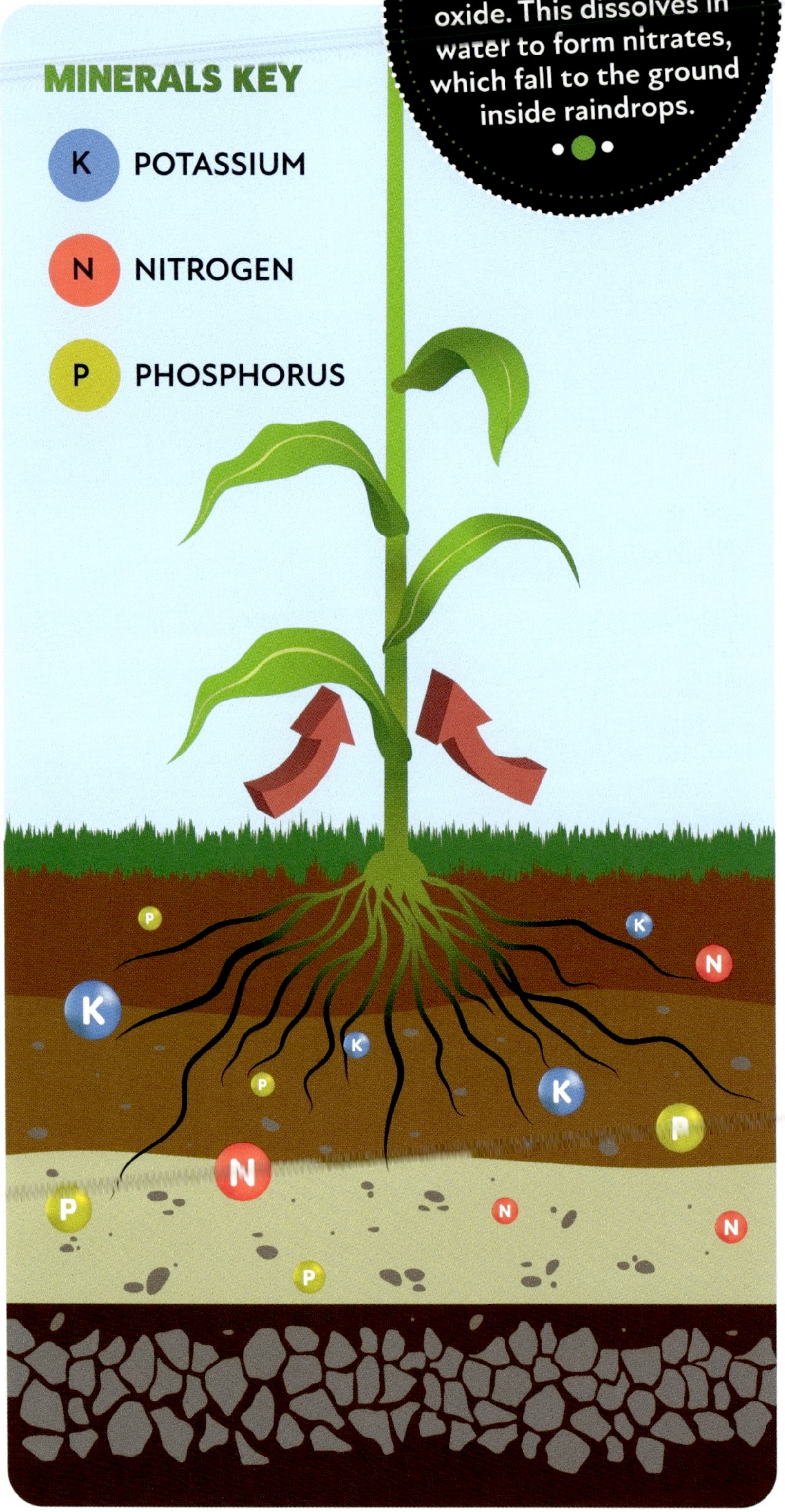

MINERALS KEY

- K POTASSIUM
- N NITROGEN
- P PHOSPHORUS

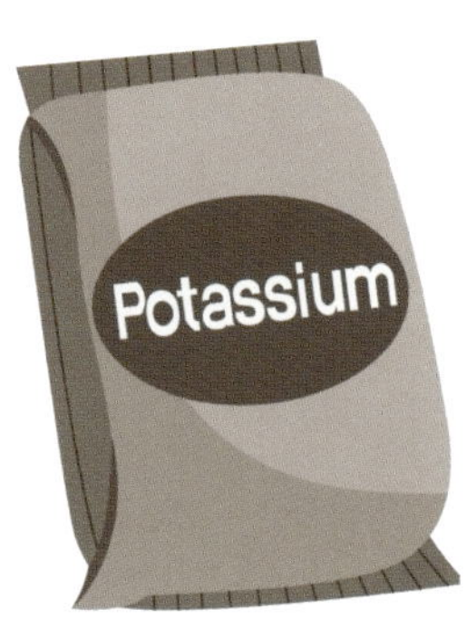

Which food?

In our gardens and on farms, we can add nutrients to the soil by applying fertiliser like cow or chicken poo. The type of fertiliser used depends on the type of plants you are trying to grow. Applying the right type and amount of fertiliser is important, as too much of a nutrient may kill the plant or cause it to grow poorly.

Rain after fire

Nutrients are added to the soil by leaves, wood and animal waste on the soil surface that are broken down by fungi, bacteria, and small animals such as earthworms. Rain washes those nutrients back into the soil, where they can be taken up again by the plants. This is called the nutrient cycle. Wildfires also add nutrients to the soil by turning leaves and wood into ash. If there is good rainfall after a fire, the extra nutrients from the ash can cause a flush of new growth.

FIRE NEAR WARWICK, QLD

Colour tells a story

Different plants need different amounts of nutrients to thrive. If even one of the nutrients is not available in the amount needed, the plant will not grow well. People who grow plants for a living can often tell which nutrients are missing by the colour of the plant's leaves. In a plant that normally has green leaves, a lack of iron will make young leaves look yellow in between bright green veins. Lack of phosphorous will turn the edges of the leaves purple.

Sandy soil

The nutrients plants take up depend partly on the type of soil plants are growing in. For example, nutrients don't stick to sand particles as well as they stick to clay, so sandy soils tend to have less nutrients than clay soils.

DID YOU KNOW?

A nutrient is a substance needed for growth and good health. 'Nutrient' comes from a Latin word meaning feed. The word 'macro' comes from a Greek word meaning large. 'Micro' comes from a Greek word meaning small.

Soil mates

Some plants (like wattles) use special bacteria in the soil to help them get more nitrogen. These bacteria live inside little lumps (called nodules) on the roots of the plant. The plant provides the bacteria with sugars for energy, and the bacteria use the energy to turn nitrogen gas from the air into a form of nitrogen the plants can take up from the soil.

Low-nutrient soils

Wild plants have developed some special adaptations to help them get more nutrients when the supply in the soil is low. One of the ways they do this is by working with a special group of fungi called mycorrhizal fungi. These fungi live partly in the plant's roots and partly in the soil; they help the plant take up water and nutrients from the soil and, in return, take some of the sugars the plant produces.

DID YOU KNOW?

When black wattle flowers in the Tiwi Islands of the Northern Territory, the islanders know to find turtles and terns eggs. The bark from this wattle is also used to make dugout canoes.

Catching flies

Plants don't just rely on fungi to help them survive in nutrient-poor soil. Some plants consume other organisms! Carnivorous plants, such as the Albany pitcher plant (*Cephalotis follicularis*) or Australia's many sundews (*Drosera* spp.), capture and digest insects in order to survive.

FACT

A mushroom is a type of fungus.

DID YOU KNOW?

The flowers of the firewood banksia (*Banksia menziesii*) were used by the Noongar people of South West Western Australia to make a sweet drink that could be used to treat sore throats.

Feathery roots

Australian soils have low levels of phosphorous, so some plants have developed specialised roots called cluster roots to help them absorb as much phosphorous as possible. These roots have many tiny hairs growing close together that make them look a bit like feathers. Cluster roots are common in our native banksia and hakea species.

Different climates

The word climate means the usual pattern of weather in an area, measured over a long period of time. This includes the highest and lowest temperatures at different times of the year and the amount of rain that falls in different months.

FACT

Temperatures have increased by more than one degree since 1960.

Climates galore

Australia is a big country and has many different types of climate – from hot and wet in Far North Queensland, to hot and dry in Alice Springs, and cold and snowy on Mount Kosciuszko. Each climate zone has a unique group of plants adapted to the local temperature and rainfall, as well as other regular events such as snowfall, drought or fire. Some plants are able to thrive in a few different climate regions, while others thrive only in a very particular climate.

ORMISTON POUND, NT
Known as Kwartatuma, this is a sacred place for the Western Arrente people.

DID YOU KNOW?

To thrive in nature, plants must be adapted to the climate and also to the particular habitat they live in. Some plants are very tough and can grow in different habitats as well as different climate zones. Others will grow well only in a very particular set of conditions.

Hot, cold, wet, dry

Plants that grow in tropical Cairns are adapted to warm temperatures all year round, very high rainfall in summer and a dry period in winter. Plants that grow in the desert near Alice Springs have adapted to high temperatures in summer and low rainfall all year round. Plants that grow in the Snowy Mountains have adapted to cool temperatures in summer and temperatures below zero in winter; on the higher parts of these mountains, plants can be completely buried under snow for several months of the year.

Habitats

A habitat is the natural home of a plant or animal. Each different habitat has features that are the result of the local climate and things like the shape of the land and nearness to fresh water or salt water. Within each climate zone, there can be many different habitats. For example, in the tropical zone, you can have forests, woodlands, wetlands, saltmarshes, and cooler areas on mountain tops. Similar habitats can be found in other climate zones.

AUSTRALIA'S HABITATS

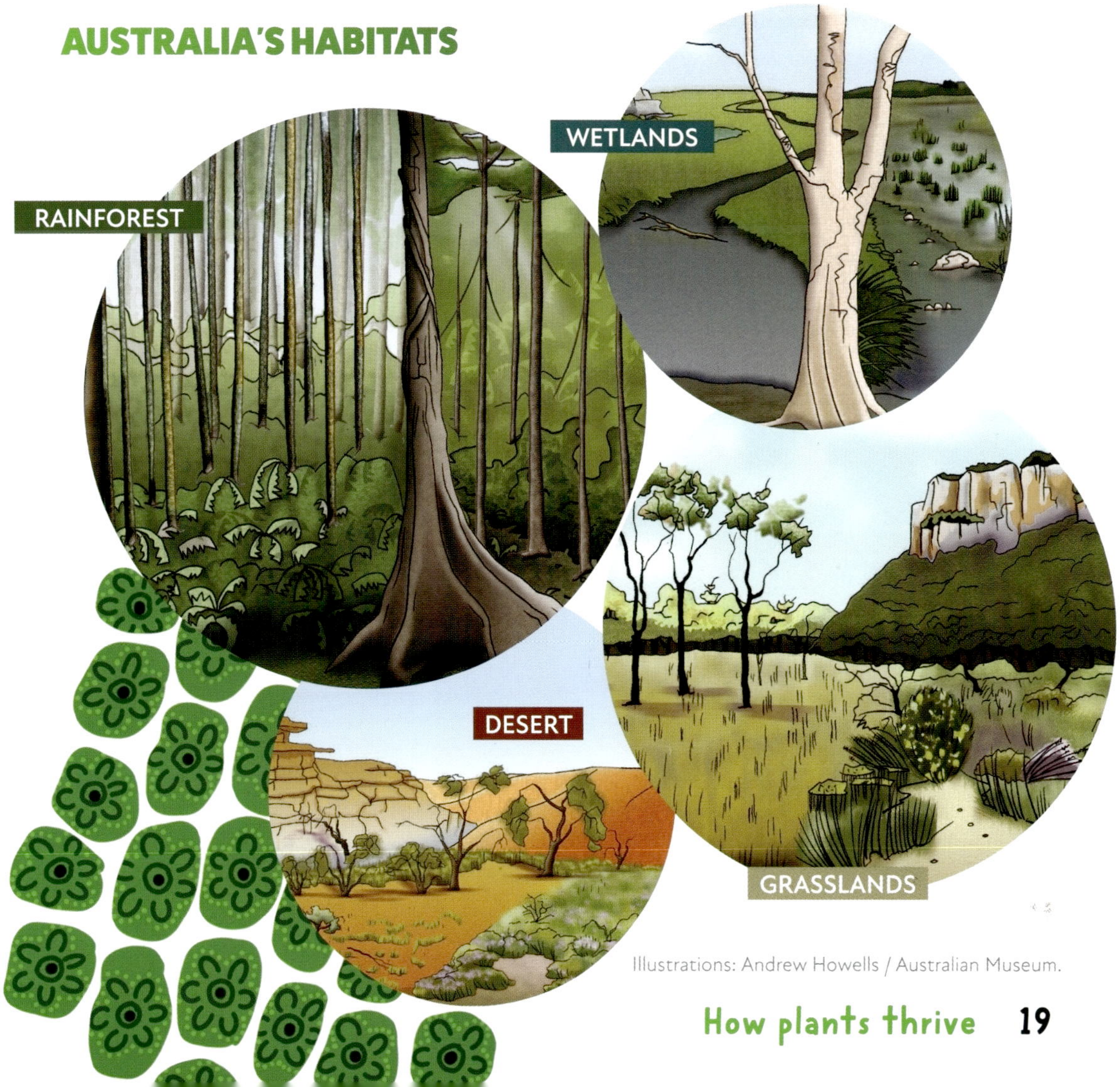

RAINFOREST

WETLANDS

DESERT

GRASSLANDS

Illustrations: Andrew Howells / Australian Museum.

Wet tropics

Plants that grow in wet tropical regions have warm temperatures all year round and plenty of water, so trees can grow very tall and form lush rainforests. Rainforest trees tend to have shallow roots, since all the moisture and nutrients they need are near the soil surface. To make up for not having deep roots, many of the taller trees have large above-ground roots called buttress roots to help keep them upright.

WET TROPICS, QLD

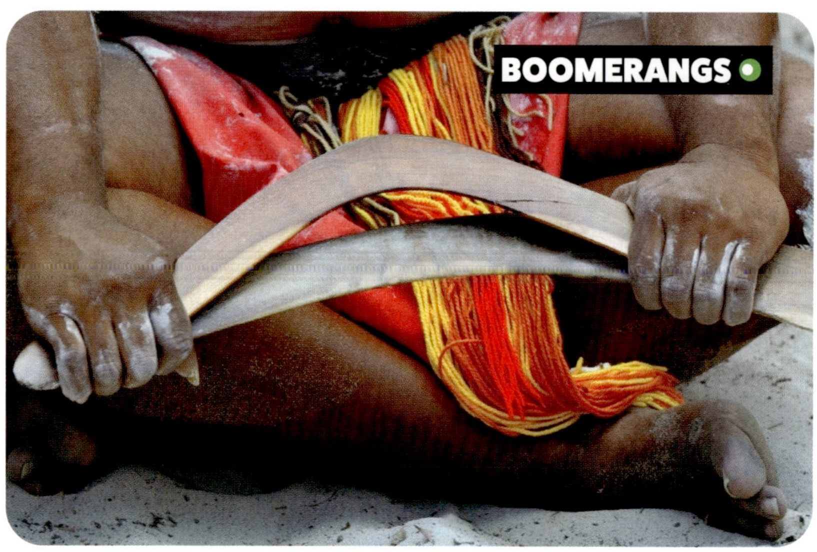

BOOMERANGS

DID YOU KNOW?

The Wik people of northern Queensland used the natural curve on buttress roots of the wild prune to make boomerangs. Wild prune (*Sersalisia sericea*) is known as yuk maak in the Wik language.

Low light

Plants growing underneath rainforest trees have to compete for light. As you saw in the section on light, plants growing in low light have adaptations that help them get as much light as possible. In rainforests, this might mean having very large leaves or having modified leaves or stems that help them climb up other plants. In tropical monsoon regions (which have alternating very dry and very wet seasons), some rainforest plants are deciduous. This means they drop their leaves in the dry season and become dormant (inactive) to survive the lack of water.

CUNJEVOI

Softly, softly

The leaves of rainforest trees tend to be soft, as they don't need to avoid drying out, and are held horizontally so that they can capture more light for photosynthesis. These leaves also often have a shiny, smooth surface and a long tip so water falling on the leaf drains quickly onto the ground.

Deserts

Plants that grow in the desert have to survive with very little water. These plants tend to be short-lived and have adaptations that help them either store water or reduce the amount of water lost from their leaves.

Hot stuff

Succulent (fleshy) stems and leaves help the plant to take up water during occasional wet periods and store it for use during dry periods. Silver-coloured leaves help to reflect heat and keep the leaves cooler. Hairs on leaves, especially around the stomata, can trap water evaporating from the leaf surface, which helps to stop more water from evaporating. Leaves reduced to tiny scales or spines can also limit water loss.

KALGOORLIE, WA

RUBY SALTBUSH

This salt-adapted succulent is known as kurrkuty in the Wemba Wemba language of north-western Victoria. Its edible berries can be made into a sweet drink and its leaves used as a flavouring.

Desert oldies

Some plants that have adapted to living in desert conditions manage to survive for a very long time. In the Mojave Desert, in the USA, the Joshua tree (*Yucca brevifolia*) can live for more than 1000 years.

STURT'S DESERT PEA

Quick bloomers

Other plants deal with a lack of water by having short lives – these plants grow, flower, set seed and die during brief rainy seasons. Their seed then lies dormant (inactive) in the soil – sometimes for many years – until the next rainy season wakes them up; they germinate and grow to maturity when the conditions mean they have a chance of survival.

DID YOU KNOW?

Succulents get their name from the Latin word 'sucus', which means juice or sap.

WILGA
This plant is called dhiil in the Gamilaraay language.

DID YOU KNOW?
Wilga (*Geijera parviflora*) is a small tree that grows in dry areas in NSW and Queensland. The leaves of this tree were used to make medicines, while the wood was used to make boomerangs.

FACT
There are more than 900 native species of eucalypt in Australia. Eucalyptus trees can even be found in the Philippines.

Dry

In places that are dry, but not as dry as the desert, trees are able to grow and plants live for longer. Trees in these habitats don't grow as tall as rainforest trees, however, and they often have tough, leathery leaves to reduce water loss. They may also have leaves that hang vertically (as many eucalyptus leaves do), which reduces the amount of sunlight hitting the leaves and reduces water lost by transpiration.

PEPPERMINT GUM

Cold

Plants that grow in the highest parts of the Snowy Mountains have to cope with very cold temperatures, frost, being buried under snow, and strong winds.

SNOW GUMS

DID YOU KNOW?

Snow gums (*Eucalyptus pauciflora*) can grow up to 20 m high in warmer areas, but they grow more like a shrub – with many stems – in the bitterly cold Snowy Mountains.

BEN LOMOND NP, TAS

FACT

The seeds of some alpine plants need to be buried under snow for several months before they will germinate.

Sleepy time

In order to survive in colder temperatures, many plants enter a kind of hibernation, just like some animals do. In the plant world, this is called dormancy. It happens when the temperature drops and the days become shorter, reducing the amount of light available to the plant. Less light and lower temperatures mean the plant can't make enough sugars through photosynthesis to fuel its growth. Dormant plants aren't completely asleep; they take the opportunity to do a little bit of maintenance. While they're resting, plants perform little jobs such as breaking down and remaking proteins, and maintaining their cell membranes.

Cold and carnivorous

First discovered on Mount Arthur, Tasmania, the tiny alpine sundew (*Drosera arcturi*) is an incredible carnivorous plant that can survive snowy conditions. It is found throughout the Australian Alps and also in New Zealand, and it blooms with a pretty white flower in summer.

ALPINE SUNDEW

Salty

Salty habitats occur in the ocean and in coastal areas where ocean tides flow onto land or mix with fresh water from rivers and creeks. They can also occur in dry inland areas where evaporation of water from the soil brings salt to the surface.

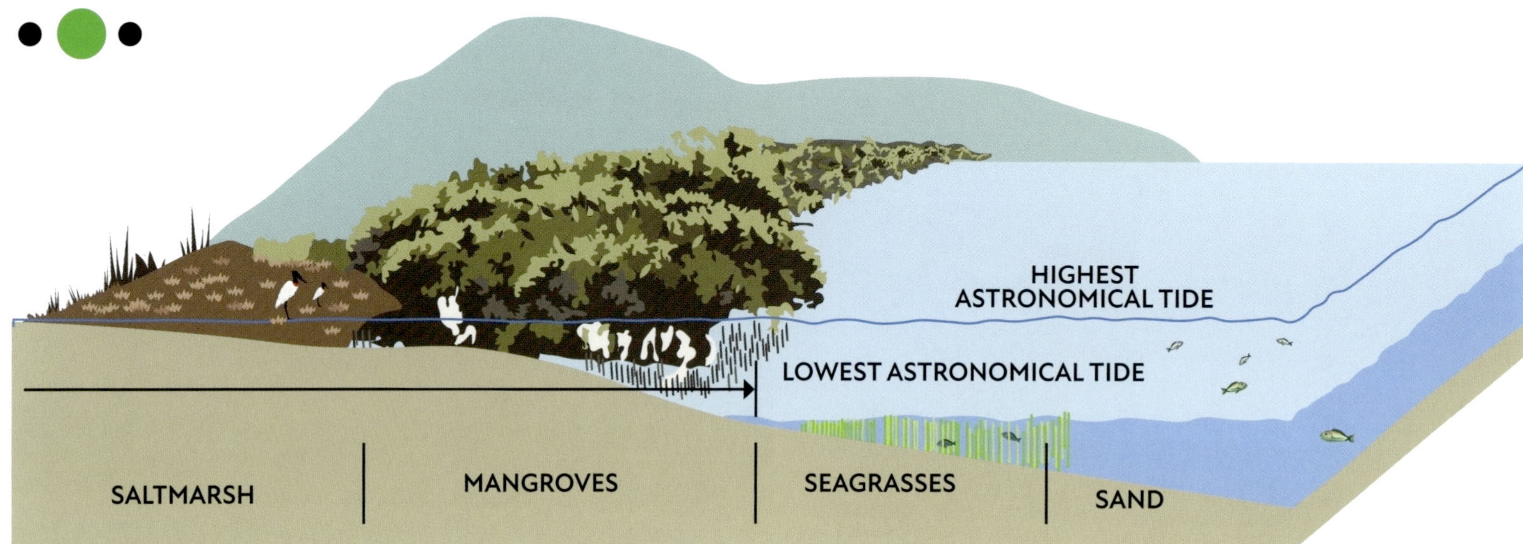

By the sea

Three groups of plants that occur in salty coastal areas are seagrasses, mangroves and saltmarshes. Seagrasses are herbs that grow under shallow water close to the shore. Mangroves are trees that grow in sand or mud at the shoreline. Saltmarshes are made up of small herbs, grasses and shrubs that grow on slightly higher ground behind the mangroves. While the roots and leaves of seagrasses are always under water, the roots of mangroves and saltmarsh plants (and sometimes the leaves of saltmarsh plants) are only under water during high tides. When development occurs, the loss of coastal habitat can be devastating. Seawalls are often constructed to protect property from potential damage caused by wave and wind action, but the natural protection given by intertidal zones allows marine life to flourish.

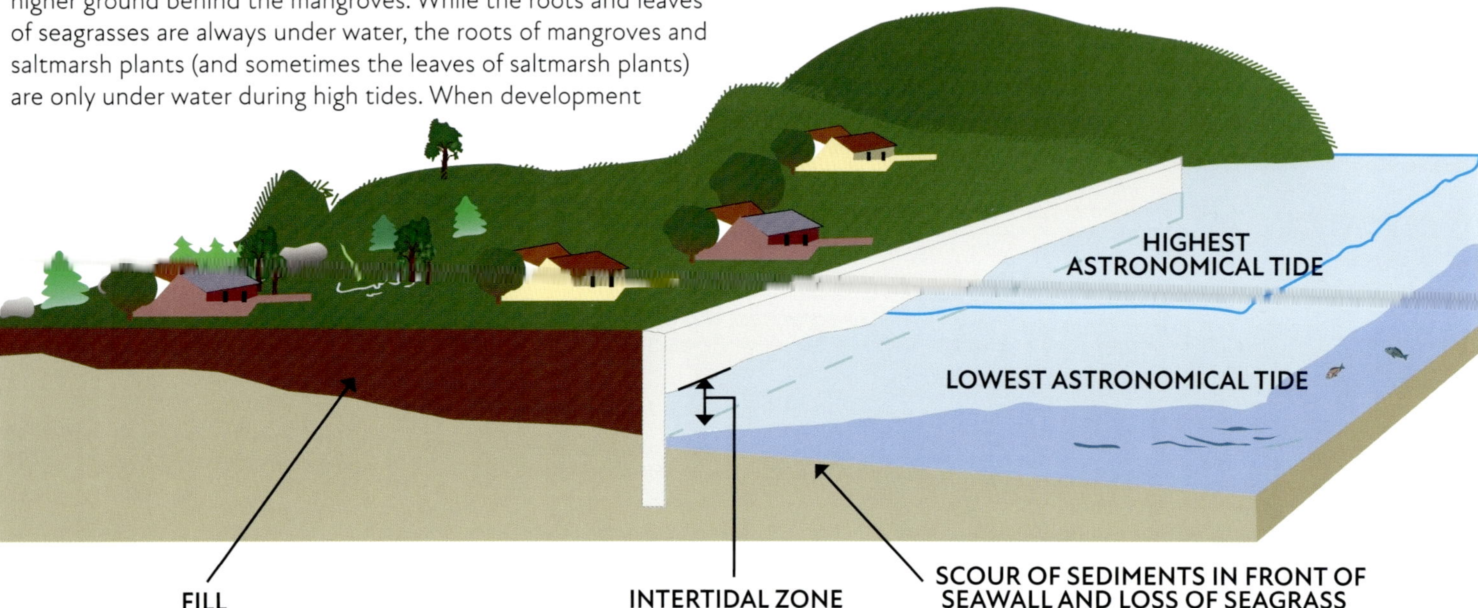

Salty plants

There are very few plants that can live in salty habitats. Those that can survive best are called halophytes. Halophytes have special adaptations to deal with salt – they can stop the salt from being taken up by their roots; they can store the salt in special compartments in their cells (called vacuoles); or they can push the salt onto their leaf surfaces through salt glands.

SEA GRASS

FACT

The word halophyte is made up of 'halo', meaning salt, and 'phyte', meaning plant.

DID YOU KNOW?

Some seagrass meadows are large enough to be seen from space! And just one square metre of seagrass can produce 10 litres of oxygen in a single day!

Learning to survive

Some plants have adapted to living in a salty environment by developing special glands near the leaf surface that can be used to store and get rid of salt. Some salt glands look like balloons and burst when full, leaving visible deposits of salt on the surface of the leaf.

RIVER MANGROVE

Fire-prone habitat

EPICORMIC GROWTH

Many Australian habitats experience bushfire. Plants growing there have two main ways to survive – by seed or by resprouting (or epicormic growth). Some plants that reproduce via seed, such as wattles, have a very hard outer seed covering. These seeds can lie dormant in the soil for years until the heat of a fire cracks the seedcoat and allows them to grow.

DID YOU KNOW?

Plants that survive by resprouting have stored food reserves in small areas under the bark or on the roots that can produce new shoots once the fire has passed.

HEATH BANKSIA
The Cadigal name for this plant is wad-ang-gari.

Pick-me-up

One glorious-looking plant is the heath banksia (*Banksia ericifolia*). Cadigal people of the Sydney region used the nectar-filled flowers of this banksia to make a sweet, high-energy drink. The flowers were soaked in water in a bowl made from bark or wood until the nectar leached out into the drink.

Coast wattle is wadanguli in the Cadigal language.

Hard to crack

The hard black seeds of the coast wattle (*Acacia longifolia*) will only germinate when fire, or having spent a long period of time in the soil, creates a crack in the seed coat that allows the seed to absorb water.

No chlorophyll

Some plants don't have chlorophyll so can't capture sunlight at all. These plants have adaptations to help them obtain food, since they can't make their own.

Crafty bloomers

Ngunnawal people could eat the tubers of the blotched hyacinth orchid (*Dipodium punctatum*) all year round because Ngunnawal women knew how to find them, even when the plant wasn't flowering.

BLOTCHED HYACINTH ORCHID

SOUTH COAST UNDERGROUND ORCHID

Photograph: Fred Hort.

FACT
Plants that don't have chlorophyll are parasites. This means they steal their food from other plants!

Fungus friend

The Western underground orchid (*Rhizanthella gardneri*) is one plant that has no chlorophyll. This plant grows and flowers entirely underground! Since it never sees the sun, the plant can't produce its own food. Instead, the orchid forms a relationship with a special soil fungus. The fungus draws food from the roots of other plants and nutrients from the breakdown of dead plants, and it transfers these to the roots of the orchid.

DID YOU KNOW?

Australia has many species of hyacinth orchid (*Dipodium* spp.) that don't have any leaves. This makes them partly reliant on their relationship with a specific soil fungus to get their nutrients.

No soil

Some plants grow on top of other plants rather than growing in the soil. These are known as epiphytes. Epiphytes include ferns, orchids, mosses and lichens – they are most common in rainforests where you can often see many different types growing on a single tree. These plants use the host plant for support and absorb water and nutrients from rainwater, mostly through their leaves rather than the roots.

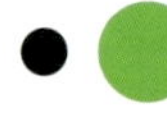

MISTLETOEBIRD

DID YOU KNOW?

Mistletoe birds eat the fruit of native mistletoe species. When the bird poops, it has to wipe its butt on a branch to get rid of the seed!

DOVE ORCHID

Sucking up

Some plants are parasites, meaning they get their water and nutrients – and sometimes their food – from a living host. Mistletoes are good examples of this adaptation. They have chlorophyll in their leaves, so they can manufacture their own food, but they take water and nutrients from a host plant.

CREEPING MISTLETOE

Photograph: Margaret R Donald.

Quiet invader

Creeping mistletoe (*Muellerina eucalyptoides*) grows on eucalypts and has leaves that are similar in shape and colour to those trees. They grow from seed deposited on a tree branch by a mistletoe bird; when the seed germinates, it grows roots into the host plant.

Waterlogged soil

Plants that grow in soil need to have oxygen around their roots. This oxygen allows root cells to burn sugar, which gives roots the energy needed to grow and take up more nutrients.

Snorkel roots

When plants are growing close to water – as in saltmarshes and mangroves – the soil can be so full of water that there is no space for oxygen. This type of soil is called waterlogged. Plants that can thrive in this habitat have special adaptations that help them get oxygen to their roots. Mangroves have many little snorkel roots called pneumatophores. These roots poke up above the surface of the soil and let the plant take in oxygen directly from the air when the tide is low.

WATER LILY STEMS

GREY MANGROVE

Air stems

Another way plants cope with waterlogged soil is by growing large air spaces inside their stems and roots. This spongy tissue – called aerenchyma – allows oxygen to pass from the shoots to the roots. Aerenchyma also helps to keep the leaves of water plants afloat so they can absorb sunlight.

Water lilies were an important food source for Indigenous people. The Thaayorre people in northern Queensland ate the roots, seeds and inner stems of the violet water lily (*Nymphaea violacea*).

VIOLET WATER LILY

DID YOU KNOW?

Aerenchyma comes from Greek words 'aer', meaning air, and 'enkhuma', meaning infusion.

Salinity experiment

Dareton Public School

Students from Parna Class – Stage 3 at Dareton Public School, in the Sunraysia area of south-west NSW – conducted a scientific experiment, using just salt, water and spinach, to show the damaging effect salt has on most plants.

Plants have a lot more to them than we think. Not only do they provide us with oxygen, they also feed us. Let's find out what happens to them when you add salt!

Materials

YOU WILL NEED –

- 4 cups, jars or bowls of water – big enough to hold 500 ml
- 2 L water
- 7 tsp salt
- 4 bunches of spinach (baby spinach with roots is best, but silverbeet or chard will work also)

Steps

STEP 1
Label each of the four containers with the numbers 1, 2, 3 and 4.

STEP 2
Pour 500 ml of water into each container.

STEP 3
Add 1 tsp salt (approximately 5 g) to container 1. Add 2 tsp salt (approximately 10 g) to container 2. Add 4 tsp salt (approximately 20 g) to container 3. Do not add any salt to container 4. It should hold water only.

STEP 4
Place one bunch of spinach or stalk of silverbeet into each container.

WHAT THIS SHOWS

This experiment demonstrates the damaging effect salt has on vegetables.

Results

Write down what each bunch of spinach or stalk of silverbeet looks like. Describe its position, colour and any other observations you make. Take some photos if you have a camera or phone handy.

BUNCH 1: Some wilting of spinach.

BUNCH 2: Wilting of spinach – more than bunch 1.

BUNCH 3: A lot of wilting of spinach – more than bunches 1 and 2.

BUNCH 4: Little wilting of spinach, if any at all.

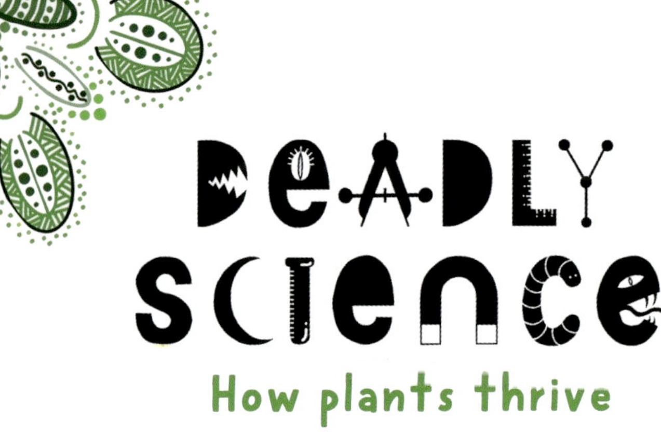

Picture credits

Front Cover: (Clockwise from top) ImageFlow/Shutterstock (SS); New Africa/SS; Photoonography/SS; captureandcompose/SS; Ezume Images/SS; Melinda Hooper; mastersky/SS; wawritto/SS; wasanajai/SS. **1.** Corey Tutt/Deadly Science. **2:** Crystal Egan/SS; Teguh Mujiono/SS; angnokever/SS. **3:** Kletr/SS; GraphicsRF.com/SS. **4:** mariokeeneye/SS; VectorMine. **5:** Marc Bruxelle/SS; SlowmotionGli/Dreamstime; Zhabska T./SS. **6:** Anne Powell/SS. **7:** Jennifer M Piper/SS; E.A Given/SS; P.j.Hickox/SS. **8:** alybaba/SS. **9:** Nataliya Hora/SS; Pawel Papis/SS; Anna Kazantseva/SS.**10:** AustralianCamera/SS; Renae Grace 333/SS; Crystal Egan/SS. **11:** vkilikov/SS; Leah-Anne Thompson/SS. **12:** BlueRingMedia/SS. **13:** Irina Khudolly/SS. **14:** Andre Adams/SS; Phuriwatt Seesuk/SS. **15:** Jen Watson/SS; Sarah2/SS; Melinda Hooper. **16:** KAVIN PHONGSATANAKORN/SS. **17:** Emna538292/SS; Serge Goujon/SS; Anne Powell/SS; galang wibowo/SS; Chris de Blank/SS. **18:** kwest/SS. **19:** AustralianCamera/SS; (c)Andrew Howells **20:** Alex Cimbal/SS; ChameleonsEye/SS; Herman Vlad/SS. **21:** Isha Photography/SS; Image Vixen/SS; AlecTrusler2015/SS. **22:** emamiel62/SS; Robyn Mackenzie/SS. **23:** Kevin Wells Photography/SS; FiledImage/SS; Vision Wildlife/SS. **24:** Australian Geographic. **25:** Rich Carey/SS; ENVIROSENSE/SS; Melinda Hooper. **26:** Boyd Martin/SS; Taras Vyshnya/SS. **27:** Ken Griffiths/SS; Fred Hort/Flickr. **28:** Aquart Designs/SS; Imogen Warren/SS. **29:** Margaret R Donald; Miliausha_art/SS. **30:** HollyHarry/SS; Sakhorn/SS; Ivonne Wierink/SS. **31:** Chones/SS; All Dareton Public School.

Hardie Grant acknowledges the Traditional Owners of the Country on which we work, the Wurundjeri People of the Kulin Nation and the Gadigal People of the Eora Nation, and recognises their continuing connection to the land, waters and culture. We pay our respects to their Elders past and present.

Hardie Grant Children's Publishing
Wurundjeri Country
Level 11, 36 Wellington Street
Collingwood Victoria 3066
Melbourne | Sydney | San Francisco
hardiegrant.com/childrens
www.australiangeographic.com.au
ISBN: 9781761217982
First published 2022
This edition published 2026

Series Editor Corey Tutt **Writer** Karen Sommerville
Illustrations Mim Cole / Mimmim

Publisher Penelope White **Editor** Savannah Hollis
Cover design Andy Warren **Internal design** Hannah Janzen
Production Sally Davis

Printed in China by LEO Paper Products LTD

The paper this book is printed on is from FSC® certified forests and other controlled sources. FSC® promotes environmentally responsible, socially beneficial and economically viable management of the world's forests.

10 9 8 7 6 5 4 3 2 1

A catalogue record for this book is available from the National Library of Australia